INTERACTIVE WHITEBOARD ACTIVITIES

SCHOLASTIC

M000121974

25 COMMON CORE MATH LESSONS
for the Interactive Whiteboard

Ready-to-Use, Animated PowerPoint® Lessons With Leveled Practice Pages That Help Students Learn and Review Key Common Core Math Concepts

by Steve Wyborney

New York ○ Toronto ○ London ○ Auckland ○ Sydney
New Delhi ○ Mexico City ○ Hong Kong ○ Buenos Aires

Teaching Resources

For Hank and Chuck—
my brothers, my friends,
my heroes.

About the CD The PowerPoint files in the attached CD are in .ppsx format. They can be opened with PowerPoint 2007 or later. If your PC does not have PowerPoint, you can download and install the free PowerPoint Viewer, which allows you to view full-featured presentations created in PowerPoint 97 and later versions.

Editor: Maria L. Chang
Cover design by Scott Davis
Interior design by Grafica Inc.

ISBN: 978-0-545-48616-3
Copyright © 2014 by Steve Wyborney
All rights reserved.
Printed in the U.S.A.

1 2 3 4 5 6 7 8 9 10   40   20 19 18 17 16 15 14

Table of Contents

The numbers in parentheses refer to corresponding PowerPoint lessons on the CD.

Welcome to *25 Common Core Math Lessons for the Interactive Whiteboard*!

The landscape around mathematical instruction is rapidly changing. Thanks to the Common Core State Standards, students and educators will learn and experience mathematical content in a different way. Many educators, schools, and districts are beginning new journeys in response to these changes and are seeking new resources—perhaps the reason you now have this book in your hands. It is my hope that this book will be a vital, powerful resource in your classroom.

This unique resource combines ready-to-use PowerPoint® lessons for your interactive whiteboard with reproducible, leveled practice sheets. The lessons place you, the classroom teacher, squarely at the center of the resource. I am certain you will feel that when you begin using it. This resource empowers you during the instructional sequence by providing visual prompts, animations, questions, and response/feedback opportunities that are completely paced by you.

The purposeful animation in the lessons is designed to make the math concepts listed in the standards more accessible to students. I fully recognize that animation can provide either clarity or distraction. For this reason, these lessons have been carefully crafted so that the animation works to simplify and illuminate mathematical concepts that students might otherwise find difficult to understand.

Thank you for including *25 Common Core Math Lessons for the Interactive Whiteboard* among your resources. I know that the resources we all treasure are the ones that make our lives simpler and our students' learning clearer. That is exactly what I believe this resource will be for you.

Kind regards,

Steve Wyborney

How to Use This Book

25 Common Core Math Lessons for the Interactive Whiteboard has been designed with whole-class instruction in mind; however, the lessons can also be used with individual students or with small groups.

This book features 25 PowerPoint lessons that support the Common Core State Standards for Mathematics. Each lesson is animated to bring clarity to a particular standard. While every lesson is complete, you might find it useful to go back and focus on a portion of a lesson to explore a particular question in greater depth. You can also use the lessons to preview upcoming content before teaching. Some of the strategies within the lessons may be new to you. In that case, they may serve as part of your personal professional learning journey.

Animated Lessons

The lessons in the attached CD are multi-click animation sequences that introduce standards-based math skills and concepts, such as using a number line to add and subtract numbers, understanding comparison symbols, measuring and comparing length, reading analog clocks to the nearest hour and half hour, and more. **The file names on the CD correspond to the numbers next to the lesson titles on the table of contents.** For example, 1.001.ppsx features the lesson "Counting Sets," 1.002.ppsx is "Relating Counting to Addition," and so on. Simply pop the CD into your computer and open the desired lesson with PowerPoint. For whole-class instruction, connect your computer to the interactive whiteboard or to a projector in front of a blank screen.

As you click (or otherwise advance) through a PowerPoint lesson and watch the animation unfold, you will find many opportunities to direct questions to your students. In general, each lesson advances from simpler, foundational concepts toward more complex concepts. Likewise, the pacing of the lesson also increases from beginning to end.

> **TIP**
>
> Since teacher mobility can sometimes be limited when using interactive whiteboards, I recommend that you acquire some type of presentation remote to advance the animations. Having a presentation remote will allow you to move easily throughout your classroom during instruction. If you don't have one, you can still use your interactive whiteboard or a wireless mouse.

The Script

Each lesson comes with a running script at the bottom of the screen. (The CD also contains a printable version of each script as a PDF file.) You can use the script in many different ways. One option is to read the script as you click through the lesson. The text has been carefully timed to correlate with the lesson's purposeful animation. Of course, you may also opt not to use the script at all, choosing to use different phrasing from what's in the lesson.

You can also use the script as a guide to help you prepare for the lesson content. As you preview the lesson, you can read through the script to better understand the timing of the animation as well as the sequence and pacing of the lesson. I predict you will use the script at some points and then veer away from it at other points where you sense opportunities for more in-depth conversations with your students.

Later, students who might benefit from a review could go through the lessons on their own—individually, in pairs, or in small groups. Simply sit them in front of a computer and allow them to click through the slideshow at their own pace, using the script to help them recall the lesson.

···· **TIP** ················

Before presenting a lesson to the whole class, review it a few times so you can see the progression of the lesson and read the script.

Lightning Round and Closing Question

Some lessons include a Lightning Round near the end of the slideshow. The slides in this section are marked by a lightning bolt and function in a similar way to flash cards. The Lightning Round indicates that the lesson has reached a point where your students should be able to respond quickly to a given question. When you see the lightning bolt, the next click will generally present the question, and the click after that will present the answer. What happens in between those two clicks is the most important part of this round. At that point, you might ask students for predictions and explanations, guide them toward validating their reasoning, layer in additional questions, or connect content with students' lives. The last slide of each lesson features a Closing Question, which is essentially a review of the concept to ensure that students fully understand the lesson.

···· **TIP** ················

In some versions of PowerPoint, a popup toolbar may appear at the bottom left of the screen during a slideshow presentation. This toolbar is generally useful for navigating from slide to slide, but the pen, in particular, can come in handy if you want to write annotations on the screen to explain a concept further or show your work.

If the toolbar does not automatically appear on your slideshow, you can activate it by going to "PowerPoint Options," selecting "Advanced," then checking "Show popup toolbar" underneath "Slide show." (On a Mac, go to "PowerPoint Preferences," click on the "View" tab, then choose "Pop-up menu button" on the drop-down menu next to "Slide show navigation.")

Common Core Content Indicators

On every lesson, you will find indicators that reference specific Common Core State Standards for Mathematics. None of the lessons are intended to provide a comprehensive definition of any of the standards; however, they are all centered squarely on specific standards, which can be referenced by looking at the lower-right corner of the lesson's title page. For a list of all the lessons and the standards they meet, see page 8.

Reproducible Practice Pages

This book contains reproducible worksheets so students can practice their new skills independently, with a partner or small group, or as a whole class. Each lesson comes with three practice pages at levels A (below grade level), B (at grade level), and C (above grade level). While you can distribute the sheets according to students' abilities, you could also give students all three sheets at different times to reinforce the skills and concepts learned from the lesson. Use the sheets for homework, independent in-class work, practice, or review. An answer key is provided at the end of the book.

The Teacher's Role

Each lesson has been purposefully designed to connect students to the content through the teacher. This is not an electronic resource that minimizes the role of the teacher. In contrast, the instruction runs directly through you, as it should. No one knows your students better than you. Although each lesson is complete and can be taught as listed, I strongly believe that some of the best instructional opportunities will happen when you pause the lesson and pursue a question or opportunity that has been revealed. In the moments when you say, "That's an interesting question. What do you think?" or "Can you explain your thinking?" or "What is another way to think about this?" you will find excellent opportunities to guide your students toward successful and powerful mathematical learning.

Lesson Overview

Below is a list of the 25 PowerPoint lessons you'll find on the CD, including a summary and the Common Core State Standard each lesson meets. For a full description of the standards, see page 13.

1.001 Counting Sets (1.OA.C.5)

This lesson guides children to count the number of various shapes on the screen.

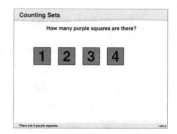

1.002 Relating Counting to Addition (1.OA.C.5)

Children review counting shapes, then explore what happens when more shapes are added. Children continue counting from the last number to arrive at the sum. They are also introduced to equations (e.g., 8 + 5 = 13).

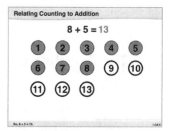

1.003 Relating Counting to Subtraction (1.OA.C.5)

With a subtraction equation as a jumping-off point, children start with a number of circles (minuend) and cross off a certain number (subtrahend) to arrive at the difference.

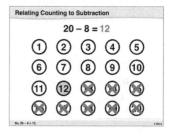

1.004 The Commutative Property of Addition (1.OA.B.3)

Using colored circles, children gain an understanding of the commutative property of addition.

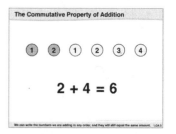

1.005 Using a Number Line to Add Two Numbers (1.OA.C.5)

Children use a number line to count to the right from the first addend to find the sum of two numbers.

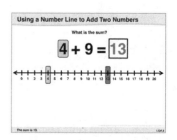

1.006 Using a Number Line to Subtract (1.OA.C.5)

Starting with the larger number in a subtraction equation, children count to the left on a number line to find the difference between two numbers.

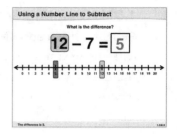

1.007 Using a Number Line to Add Three Numbers (1.OA.A.2)

As an extension to the fifth lesson, children use a number line to find the sum of three numbers.

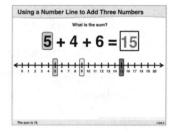

1.008 Reading & Writing Numbers Through 120 (1.NBT.A.1)

Children identify the numerals 1 to 10, then the numerals 10 to 100 in increments of 10. Next, they learn how to write number words and when to use a hyphen (for the numbers twenty-one to ninety-nine, except for numbers with a zero in the ones place), before moving on to larger numbers up to 120.

1.009 Understanding Ones and Tens Through 19 (1.NBT.B.2)

Children learn the concept of "ones" and "tens" by counting squares. As they count from one to nine, the corresponding number is written in the ones place. When they reach 10, however, they bundle the 10 squares together and think of it as "1 group of ten and 0 ones." They continue to count each additional square (up to 19) and represent the new number as "1 ten and 9 ones," for example.

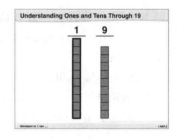

1.010 Understanding Ones and Tens in Larger Numbers (1.NBT.B.2)

After a brief review of the previous lesson, children expand on the concept of ones and tens by exploring larger numbers. Children understand that 1 ten and 10 ones is equivalent to "2 tens and 0 ones" or 20, then continue to identify larger two-digit numbers by counting the number of tens and ones.

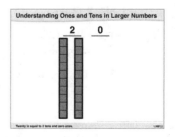

1.011 Counting Sequences Between 1 and 120 (1.NBT.A.1)

Starting with a specific number (for example, 5), children fill out a chart with the next four numbers in sequence (6, 7, 8, 9). They then refer to a hundreds chart to help them sequence larger numbers, then practice doing it without the chart.

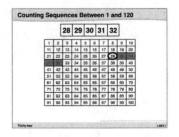

1.012 Counting to 120 From Any Number (1.NBT.A.1)

Children select a number from the first column of a hundreds chart that has been extended up to 120 and count up from that number.

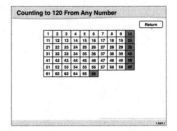

1.013 Understanding Comparison Symbols (1.NBT.B.3)

This lesson introduces children to the symbols for less than, greater than, and equal to. They then use the symbols to compare single-digit numbers.

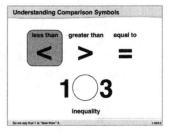

1.014 Comparing Two-Digit Numbers (1.NBT.B.3)

To compare two-digit numbers, children first look at the digits in the tens place. If the number of tens is the same for both numbers, they then look at the digits in the ones place and compare to see if the first number is greater than, less than, or equal to the second number. If the number of tens is different, however, it is not necessary to compare the ones. Simply compare the value of the tens place.

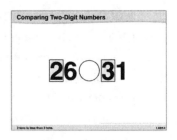

1.015 Adding a One-Digit Number to a Two-Digit Number (1.NBT.C.4)

Using a hundreds chart, children learn to count up in order to add a one-digit number to a two-digit number. For example, to solve 23 + 5, children find 23 on the hundreds chart, then count up 5 to arrive at the sum of 28.

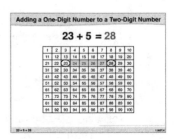

10

1.016 Adding Multiples of 10 (1.NBT.C.4)

Children review how to count up on a hundreds chart in order to add 10 to any number. They soon notice that the sum falls directly below the starting number on the hundreds chart. Children then apply this knowledge to add multiples of 10 to a number.

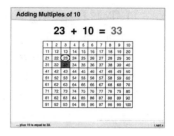

1.017 Subtracting Multiples of 10 (1.NBT.C.6)

Reversing the strategy learned from the previous lesson, children subtract 10 from a number by simply looking at the number directly above the starting number (minuend) on the hundreds chart. To subtract multiples of 10, just count by tens above the minuend.

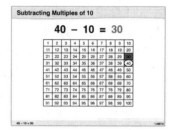

1.018 Mentally Adding & Subtracting 10 (1.NBT.C.5)

After reviewing the strategies for adding and subtracting 10 using the hundreds chart, children learn how to do it without the help of the chart. They focus on the digit in the tens place and add one more to mentally add 10 and take away one to mentally subtract 10.

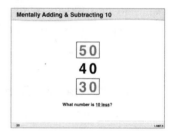

1.019 Measuring Length (1.MD.A.2)

Given a unit of length, children measure how long a shape is by laying down copies of the unit of length end-to-end across the shape and counting the units.

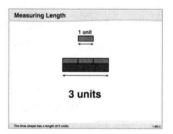

1.020 Comparing Length (1.MD.A.1)

Children measure the length of two different shapes using the same strategy learned in the previous lesson. They then compare the lengths to determine which one is longer. The lesson continues with children measuring and comparing the lengths of three shapes and ordering the shapes by length.

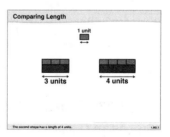

1.021 Reading Analog Clocks to the Nearest Hour (1.MD.B.3)

This lesson on how to read time starts by looking at the parts of a clock—the numbers around an analog clock, the minute hand, and the hour hand. As the clock is put in motion, children understand that when the minute hand is pointing directly to the top of the clock and the hour hand is pointing to a number, such as 6, then the time is that number—6:00.

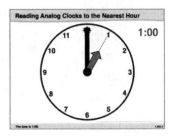

1.022 Reading Analog Clocks to the Nearest Half Hour (1.MD.B.3)

After a quick review of how to read time to the hour, children proceed to read time to the half hour. They'll see that when the minute hand is pointing directly to the bottom of the clock, the hour hand will point between two numbers, such as 12 and 1. They learn that since the hour hand is not yet at the 1, the time starts with the last number the hour hand was pointing to—in this case, 12. The minute hand pointing straight down reads as 0:30, so the time is 12:30. Children have several opportunities to practice so they become adept at this skill by the end of the lesson.

1.023 Making Shapes (1.G.A.2)

Starting with a single square, children divide the square into halves to make two rectangles, then put them back together again. Children then divide the square into fourths to make smaller squares, rearrange them to make various shapes, and discover how the new shapes look when rotated, flipped, or turned. The lesson continues to explore other shapes, such as triangles and rectangles.

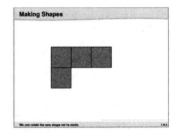

1.024 Partitioning Shapes Into Halves (1.G.A.3)

Children explore different ways to break a shape into two equal parts, or *halves*. They understand that both halves are the same size and together, they make up the whole shape.

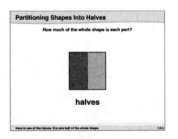

1.025 Partitioning Shapes Into Fourths (1.G.A.3)

As an extension to the previous slideshow, this lesson explores different ways to break a shape into four equal parts, also known as *fourths* or *quarters*. Children understand that each part is one-fourth of the whole shape.

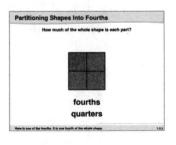

Meeting the
Common Core State Standards

The lessons and activities in this resource meet the following Common Core State Standards for Mathematics. For more information, visit the CCSSI website at **www.corestandards.org/math**.

Operations and Algebraic Thinking (1.OA)

Represent and solve problems involving addition and subtraction.
1.OA.A.2 Solve word problems that call for addition of three whole numbers whose sum is less than or equal to 20, e.g., by using objects, drawings, and equations with a symbol for the unknown number to represent the problem.

Understand and apply properties of operations and the relationship between addition and subtraction.
1.OA.B.3 Apply properties of operations as strategies to add and subtract.

Add and subtract within 20.
1.OA.C.5 Relate counting to addition and subtraction (e.g., by counting on 2 to add 2).

Work with addition and subtraction equations.
1.OA.D.8 Determine the unknown whole number in an addition or subtraction equation relating three whole numbers.

Number and Operations in Base Ten (1.NBT)

Extend the counting sequence.
1.NBT.A.1 Count to 120, starting at any number less than 120. In this range, read and write numerals and represent a number of objects with a written numeral.

Understand place value.

1.NBT.B.2 Understand that the two digits of a two-digit number represent amounts of tens and ones. Understand the following as special cases:

1.NBT.B.2a 10 can be thought of as a bundle of ten ones — called a "ten."

1.NBT.B.2b The numbers from 11 to 19 are composed of a ten and one, two, three, four, five, six, seven, eight, or nine ones.

1.NBT.B.2c The numbers 10, 20, 30, 40, 50, 60, 70, 80, 90 refer to one, two, three, four, five, six, seven, eight, or nine tens (and 0 ones).

1.NBT.B.3 Compare two two-digit numbers based on meanings of the tens and ones digits, recording the results of comparisons with the symbols >, =, and <.

Use place value understanding and properties of operations to add and subtract.

1.NBT.C.4 Add within 100, including adding a two-digit number and a one-digit number, and adding a two-digit number and a multiple of 10, using concrete models or drawings and strategies based on place value, properties of operations, and/or the relationship between addition and subtraction; relate the strategy to a written method and explain the reasoning used. Understand that in adding two-digit numbers, one adds tens and tens, ones and ones; and sometimes it is necessary to compose a ten.

1.NBT.C.5 Given a two-digit number, mentally find 10 more or 10 less than the number, without having to count; explain the reasoning used.

1.NBT.C.6 Subtract multiples of 10 in the range 10–90 from multiples of 10 in the range 10–90 (positive or zero differences), using concrete models or drawings and strategies based on place value, properties of operations, and/or the relationship between addition and subtraction; relate the strategy to a written method and explain the reasoning used.

Measurement and Data (1.MD)

Measure lengths indirectly and by iterating length units.

1.MD.A.1 Order three objects by length; compare the lengths of two objects indirectly by using a third object.

1.MD.A.2 Express the length of an object as a whole number of length units, by laying multiple copies of a shorter object (the length unit) end to end; understand that the length measurement of an object is the number of same-size length units that span it with no gaps or overlaps.

Tell and write time.

1.MD.B.3 Tell and write time in hours and half-hours using analog and digital clocks.

Geometry (1.G)

Reason with shapes and their attributes.

1.G.A.2 Compose two-dimensional shapes (rectangles, squares, trapezoids, triangles, half-circles, and quarter-circles) or three-dimensional shapes (cubes, right rectangular prisms, right circular cones, and right circular cylinders) to create a composite shape, and compose new shapes from the composite shape.

1.G.A.3 Partition circles and rectangles into two and four equal shares, describe the shares using the words *halves*, *fourths*, and *quarters*, and use the phrases *half of*, *fourth of*, and *quarter of*. Describe the whole as two of or four of the shares. Understand for these examples that decomposing into more equal shares creates smaller shares.

Name _____ Date _____

Number each set of shapes.

①
1	2	3		

②

③

④

25 Common Core Math Lessons for the Interactive Whiteboard: Grade 1 © 2014 by Steve Wyborney, Scholastic Teaching Resources

Name _____ Date _____

Number each set of shapes.

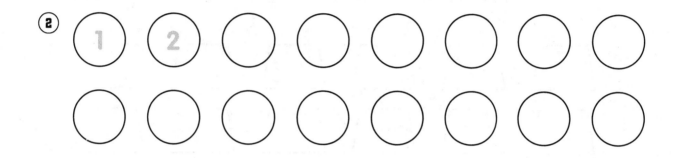

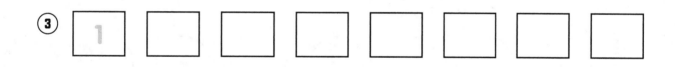

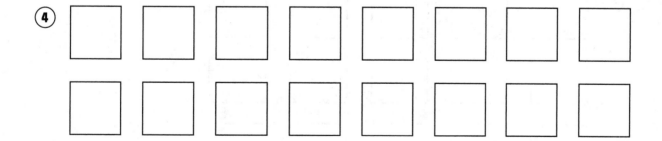

Name _____ Date _____

Number each set of shapes.

① | 1 | 2 | 3 | ☐ | ☐ | ☐ | ☐ | ☐ |

☐ ☐ ☐ ☐ ☐ ☐ ☐ ☐

② 1 2 ⬜ ⬜ ⬜ ⬜

⬜ ⬜ ⬜ ⬜ ⬜

⬜ ⬜ ⬜ ⬜ ⬜

③ 1 ○ ○ ○ ○ ○ ○ ○

④ ☐ ☐ ☐ ☐ ☐

☐ ☐ ☐ ☐ ☐

☐ ☐ ☐ ☐ ☐

☐ ☐ ☐ ☐ ☐

25 Common Core Math Lessons for the Interactive Whiteboard: Grade 1 © 2014 by Steve Wyborney, Scholastic Teaching Resources

Name _____ Date _____

Draw and count to find the sum.

①   4 + 3 = _____

②   6 + 5 = _____

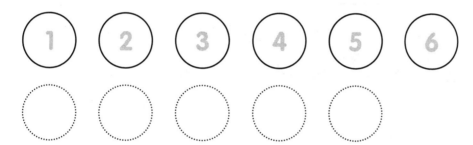

③   3 + 5 = _____

④   2 + 4 = _____

Name _____ Date _____

Draw and count to find the sum.

①   3 + 5 = _____

②   5 + 4 = _____

③   2 + 6 = _____

④   4 + 7 = _____

25 Common Core Math Lessons for the Interactive Whiteboard: Grade 1 © 2014 by Steve Wyborney, Scholastic Teaching Resources

Name _____ Date _____

Draw and count to find the sum.

①   6 + 7 = _____

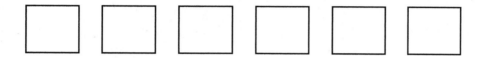

②   3 + 9 = _____

③   7 + 7 = _____

④   5 + 8 = _____

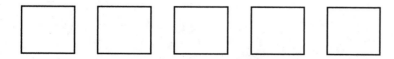

Name _____ Date _____

Count to subtract.

① $5 - 2 =$ _____

①②③④⑤ (1 2 3 4 5)

② $5 - 4 =$ _____

(1 2 3 4 5)

③ $4 - 2 =$ _____

(1 2 3 4)

④ $5 - 3 =$ _____

(1 2 3 4 5)

⑤ $10 - 3 =$ _____

(1 2 3 4 5)
(6 7 8 9 10)

⑥ $9 - 4 =$ _____

(1 2 3 4 5)
(6 7 8 9)

⑦ $10 - 7 =$ _____

(1 2 3 4 5)
(6 7 8 9 10)

⑧ $8 - 6 =$ _____

(1 2 3 4 5)
(6 7 8)

25 Common Core Math Lessons for the Interactive Whiteboard: Grade 1 © 2014 by Steve Wyborney, Scholastic Teaching Resources

Name _____ Date _____

Count to subtract.

① $8 - 5 =$ _____

① ② ③ ④ ⑤

⑥ ⑦ ⑧

② $10 - 6 =$ _____

① ② ③ ④ ⑤

⑥ ⑦ ⑧ ⑨ ⑩

③ $15 - 13 =$ _____

① ② ③ ④ ⑤

⑥ ⑦ ⑧ ⑨ ⑩

⑪ ⑫ ⑬ ⑭ ⑮

④ $12 - 4 =$ _____

① ② ③ ④ ⑤

⑥ ⑦ ⑧ ⑨ ⑩

⑪ ⑫

⑤ $20 - 16 =$ _____

① ② ③ ④ ⑤

⑥ ⑦ ⑧ ⑨ ⑩

⑪ ⑫ ⑬ ⑭ ⑮

⑯ ⑰ ⑱ ⑲ ⑳

⑥ $16 - 7 =$ _____

① ② ③ ④ ⑤

⑥ ⑦ ⑧ ⑨ ⑩

⑪ ⑫ ⑬ ⑭ ⑮

⑯

Name _____ Date _____

Count to subtract.

① $14 - 3 =$ _____

① 2 ③ ④ ⑤
⑥ ⑦ ⑧ ⑨ ⑩
⑪ ⑫ ⑬ ⑭

② $15 - 8 =$ _____

① ② ③ ④ ⑤
⑥ ⑦ ⑧ ⑨ ⑩
⑪ ⑫ ⑬ ⑭ ⑮

③ $9 - 6 =$ _____

① ② ③ ④ ⑤
⑥ ⑦ ⑧ ⑨

④ $10 - 4 =$ _____

① ② ③ ④ ⑤
⑥ ⑦ ⑧ ⑨ ⑩

⑤ $17 - 9 =$ _____

① ② ③ ④ ⑤
⑥ ⑦ ⑧ ⑨ ⑩
⑪ ⑫ ⑬ ⑭ ⑮
⑯ ⑰

⑥ $20 - 14 =$ _____

① ② ③ ④ ⑤
⑥ ⑦ ⑧ ⑨ ⑩
⑪ ⑫ ⑬ ⑭ ⑮
⑯ ⑰ ⑱ ⑲ ⑳

25 Common Core Math Lessons for the Interactive Whiteboard: Grade 1 © 2014 by Steve Wyborney, Scholastic Teaching Resources

Name _____ Date _____

Find the missing sum. Use the commutative property.

① $3 + 5 = 8$
$5 + 3 =$ _____

② $4 + 1 = 5$
$1 + 4 =$ _____

③ $7 + 2 = 9$
$2 + 7 =$ _____

④ $1 + 2 = 3$
$2 + 1 =$ _____

⑤ $5 + 2 = 7$
$2 + 5 =$ _____

⑥ $4 + 2 = 6$
$2 + 4 =$ _____

⑦ $1 + 3 = 4$
$3 + 1 =$ _____

⑧ $2 + 3 = 5$
$3 + 2 =$ _____

⑨ $4 + 5 = 9$
$5 + 4 =$ _____

⑩ $1 + 7 = 8$
$7 + 1 =$ _____

Name _____ Date _____

Find the missing sum. Use the commutative property.

① $6 + 8 = 14$

$8 + 6 =$ _____

② $9 + 2 = 11$

$2 + 9 =$ _____

③ $4 + 3 = 7$

$3 + 4 =$ _____

④ $9 + 7 = 16$

$7 + 9 =$ _____

⑤ $5 + 4 = 9$

$4 + 5 =$ _____

⑥ $7 + 5 = 12$

$5 + 7 =$ _____

⑦ $9 + 8 = 17$

$8 + 9 =$ _____

⑧ $1 + 9 = 10$

$9 + 1 =$ _____

⑨ $9 + 5 = 14$

$5 + 9 =$ _____

⑩ $10 + 6 = 16$

$6 + 10 =$ _____

25 Common Core Math Lessons for the Interactive Whiteboard: Grade 1 © 2014 by Steve Wyborney, Scholastic Teaching Resources

Name _____ Date _____

Find the missing sum. Use the commutative property.

① $9 + 5 = 14$

　$5 + 9 =$ _____

② $10 + 4 = 14$

　$4 + 10 =$ _____

③ $7 + 8 = 15$

　$8 + 7 =$ _____

④ $2 + 5 = 7$

　$5 + 2 =$ _____

⑤ $6 + 3 = 9$

　$3 + 6 =$ _____

⑥ $9 + 8 = 17$

　$8 + 9 =$ _____

⑦ $7 + 4 = 11$

　$4 + 7 =$ _____

⑧ $9 + 10 = 19$

　$10 + 9 =$ _____

⑨ $8 + 4 = 12$

　$4 + 8 =$ _____

⑩ $7 + 5 = 12$

　$5 + 7 =$ _____

Name _____ Date _____

Find the sum. Use the number line to help you.

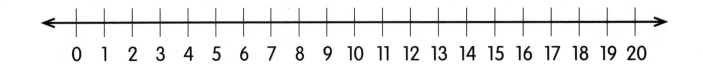

① $4 + 5 =$ ☐   ② $2 + 6 =$ ☐

③ $5 + 2 =$ ☐   ④ $4 + 7 =$ ☐

⑤ $6 + 8 =$ ☐   ⑥ $8 + 5 =$ ☐

⑦ $7 + 7 =$ ☐   ⑧ $4 + 3 =$ ☐

⑨ $3 + 8 =$ ☐   ⑩ $9 + 3 =$ ☐

⑪ $9 + 9 =$ ☐   ⑫ $4 + 8 =$ ☐

25 Common Core Math Lessons for the Interactive Whiteboard: Grade 1 © 2014 by Steve Wyborney, Scholastic Teaching Resources

Name _____ Date _____

Find the sum. Use the number line to help you.

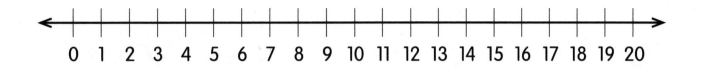

① 8 + 8 = ☐

② 7 + 6 = ☐

③ 11 + 4 = ☐

④ 3 + 15 = ☐

⑤ 8 + 6 = ☐

⑥ 7 + 5 = ☐

⑦ 4 + 12 = ☐

⑧ 12 + 3 = ☐

⑨ 11 + 7 = ☐

⑩ 5 + 5 = ☐

⑪ 6 + 5 = ☐

⑫ 4 + 15 = ☐

Name _____ Date _____

Find the sum. Use the number line to help you.

① 14 + 4 = ☐   ② 3 + 17 = ☐

③ 16 + 3 = ☐   ④ 8 + 7 = ☐

⑤ 2 + 15 = ☐   ⑥ 11 + 8 = ☐

⑦ 2 + 14 = ☐   ⑧ 9 + 6 = ☐

⑨ 5 + 8 = ☐   ⑩ 10 + 7 = ☐

⑪ 15 + 3 = ☐   ⑫ 6 + 14 = ☐

Name _____ Date _____

Find the difference. Use the number line to help you.

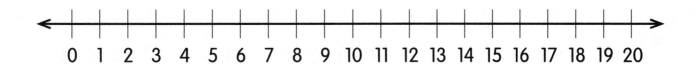

① 7 – 4 = [ ] ② 8 – 3 = [ ]

③ 9 – 8 = [ ] ④ 6 – 4 = [ ]

⑤ 12 – 4 = [ ] ⑥ 14 – 5 = [ ]

⑦ 10 – 3 = [ ] ⑧ 9 – 7 = [ ]

⑨ 18 – 6 = [ ] ⑩ 15 – 9 = [ ]

⑪ 11 – 7 = [ ] ⑫ 19 – 8 = [ ]

Name _____ Date _____

Find the difference. Use the number line to help you.

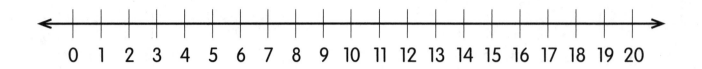

① 16 − 3 = ☐

② 9 − 6 = ☐

③ 7 − 5 = ☐

④ 14 − 11 = ☐

⑤ 17 − 12 = ☐

⑥ 12 − 8 = ☐

⑦ 16 − 6 = ☐

⑧ 8 − 5 = ☐

⑨ 15 − 3 = ☐

⑩ 14 − 7 = ☐

⑪ 18 − 6 = ☐

⑫ 20 − 9 = ☐

Name _____ Date _____

Find the difference. Use the number line to help you.

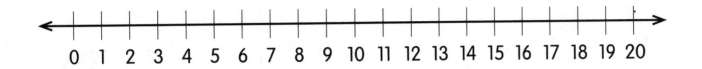

① 15 − 4 = ☐　　　② 7 − 6 = ☐

③ 9 − 4 = ☐　　　④ 17 − 10 = ☐

⑤ 18 − 14 = ☐　　　⑥ 15 − 7 = ☐

⑦ 12 − 9 = ☐　　　⑧ 19 − 4 = ☐

⑨ 18 − 12 = ☐　　　⑩ 10 − 8 = ☐

⑪ 20 − 6 = ☐　　　⑫ 20 − 15 = ☐

Name _____ Date _____

Find the sum. Use the number line to help you.

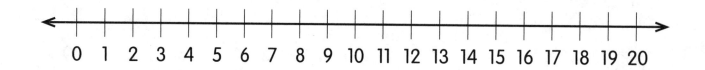

① $2 + 3 + 4 =$ ▢   ② $8 + 5 + 2 =$ ▢

③ $7 + 3 + 3 =$ ▢   ④ $2 + 6 + 3 =$ ▢

⑤ $5 + 5 + 5 =$ ▢   ⑥ $3 + 5 + 7 =$ ▢

⑦ $8 + 1 + 8 =$ ▢   ⑧ $4 + 8 + 7 =$ ▢

⑨ $1 + 6 + 1 =$ ▢   ⑩ $5 + 6 + 9 =$ ▢

⑪ $7 + 4 + 2 =$ ▢   ⑫ $4 + 3 + 3 =$ ▢

25 Common Core Math Lessons for the Interactive Whiteboard: Grade 1 © 2014 by Steve Wyborney, Scholastic Teaching Resources

Name _____ Date _____

Find the sum. Use the number line to help you.

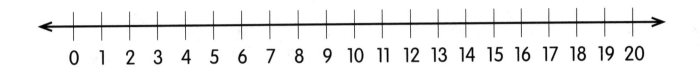

0 1 2 3 4 5 6 7 8 9 10 11 12 13 14 15 16 17 18 19 20

① $7 + 6 + 7 =$ ☐   ② $4 + 4 + 4 =$ ☐

③ $10 + 5 + 3 =$ ☐   ④ $3 + 7 + 9 =$ ☐

⑤ $8 + 4 + 5 =$ ☐   ⑥ $3 + 2 + 2 =$ ☐

⑦ $4 + 3 + 10 =$ ☐   ⑧ $9 + 2 + 9 =$ ☐

⑨ $4 + 8 + 3 =$ ☐   ⑩ $7 + 4 + 2 =$ ☐

⑪ $8 + 1 + 3 =$ ☐   ⑫ $2 + 4 + 3 =$ ☐

Name _____ Date _____

Find the sum. Use the number line to help you.

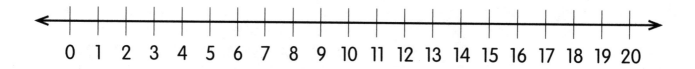

① $3 + 3 + 3 =$ ☐   ② $2 + 10 + 5 =$ ☐

③ $12 + 4 + 2 =$ ☐   ④ $5 + 3 + 11 =$ ☐

⑤ $6 + 4 + 3 =$ ☐   ⑥ $5 + 2 + 8 =$ ☐

⑦ $3 + 4 + 8 =$ ☐   ⑧ $6 + 1 + 4 =$ ☐

⑨ $1 + 3 + 3 =$ ☐   ⑩ $6 + 7 + 4 =$ ☐

⑪ $7 + 6 + 3 =$ ☐   ⑫ $2 + 2 + 3 =$ ☐

25 Common Core Math Lessons for the Interactive Whiteboard: Grade 1 © 2014 by Steve Wyborney, Scholastic Teaching Resources

Name _____ Date _____

Trace the number.

① twenty-five

_25_

② thirty-six

_36_

③ fifteen

_15_

④ forty

_40_

⑤ sixty-one

_61_

⑥ one hundred

_100_

⑦ ninety-three

_93_

⑧ six

_6_

⑨ fifty-five

_55_

⑩ eighty-four

_84_

⑪ twelve

_12_

⑫ forty-two

_42_

Name _____ Date _____

Trace the number.

① thirty-nine

_39_

② twenty-seven

_27_

③ nine

_9_

④ fifty-four

_54_

⑤ ninety-nine

_99_

⑥ one hundred two

_102_

⑦ forty-nine

_49_

⑧ fifty-one

_51_

⑨ forty-four

_44_

⑩ one hundred ten

_110_

⑪ fifteen

_15_

⑫ seventy-three

_73_

Name _____ Date _____

Write the number.

① forty-six

_____

② twenty-one

_____

③ seventy-five

_____

④ fifty-two

_____

⑤ ninety-one

_____

⑥ one hundred three

_____

⑦ seventy-six

_____

⑧ sixty-nine

_____

⑨ eighty-four

_____

⑩ one hundred twelve

_____

⑪ twenty-seven

_____

⑫ fifty-six

_____

Name _____ Date _____

Write the number that is shown.

① _____

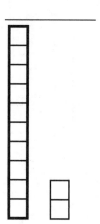

② _____

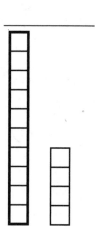

③ _____

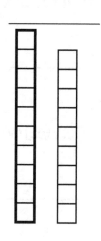

④ _____

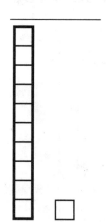

⑤ _____

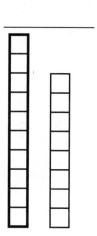

⑥ _____

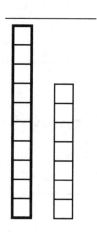

⑦ _____

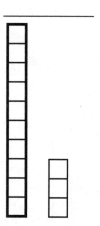

⑧ _____

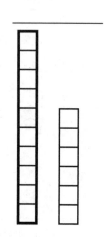

⑨ _____

Name _____ Date _____

Write the number that is shown.

① _____

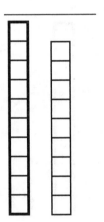

② _____

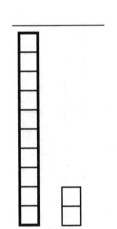

③ _____

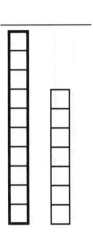

④ _____

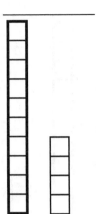

⑤ _____

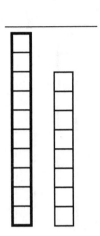

⑥ _____

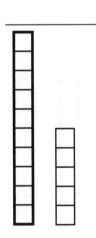

⑦ _____

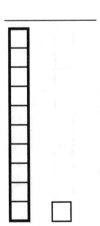

⑧ _____

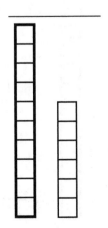

⑨ _____

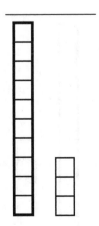

Name _____ Date _____

Write the number that is shown.

(1) _____

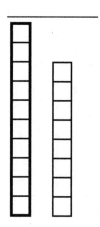

(2) _____

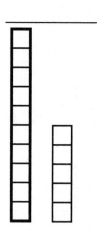

(3) _____

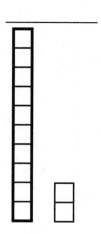

(4) _____

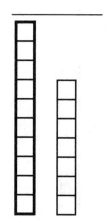

(5) _____

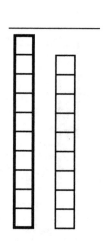

(6) _____

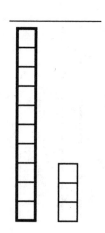

(7) _____

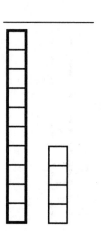

(8) _____

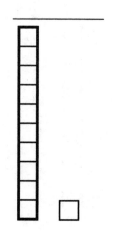

(9) _____

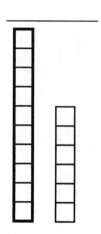

Name _____ Date _____

Write the number that is shown.

1 _____

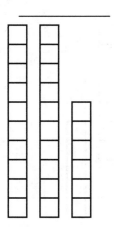

2 _____

3 _____

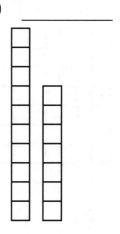

4 _____

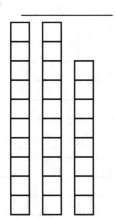

5 _____

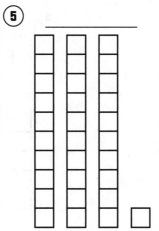

6 _____

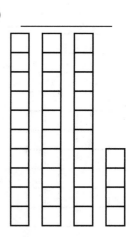

7 _____

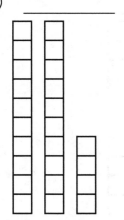

8 _____

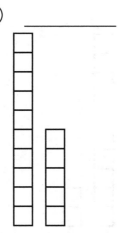

9 _____

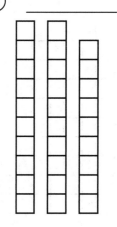

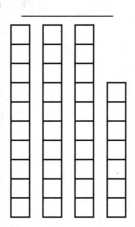

Name _____ Date _____

Write the number that is shown.

① _____

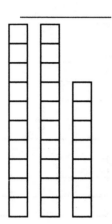

② _____

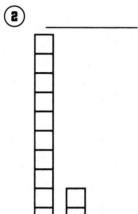

③ _____

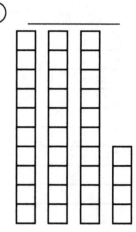

④ _____

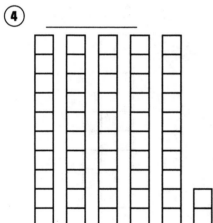

⑤ _____

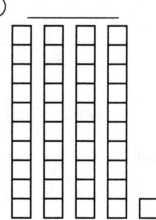

⑥ _____

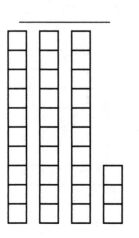

⑦ _____

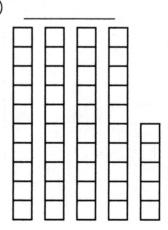

44

Name _____ Date _____

Write the number that is shown.

(1) _____

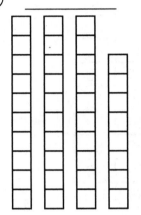

(2) _____

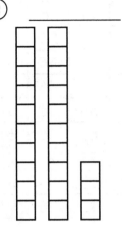

(3) _____

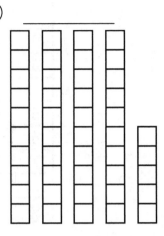

(4) _____

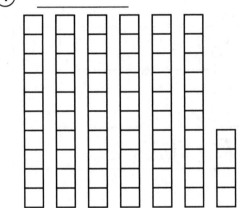

(5) _____

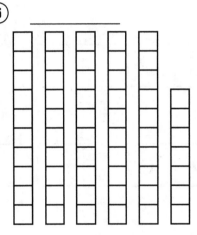

(6) _____

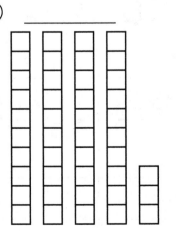

(7) _____

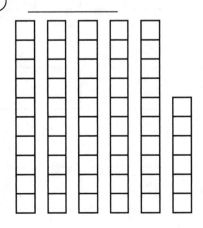

Counting Sequences
Between 1 and 120: A

Name _____ Date _____

Finish the counting charts. Use the hundreds chart to help you.

1	2	3	4	5	6	7	8	9	10
11	12	13	14	15	16	17	18	19	20
21	22	23	24	25	26	27	28	29	30
31	32	33	34	35	36	37	38	39	40
41	42	43	44	45	46	47	48	49	50
51	52	53	54	55	56	57	58	59	60
61	62	63	64	65	66	67	68	69	70
71	72	73	74	75	76	77	78	79	80
81	82	83	84	85	86	87	88	89	90
91	92	93	94	95	96	97	98	99	100

1) 21 22 __ __ __

2) 38 39 __ __ __

3) 9 10 __ __ __

4) 77 78 __ __ __

5) 45 46 __ __ __

6) 53 54 __ __ __

7) 87 88 __ __ __

8) 37 38 __ __ __

9) 13 14 __ __ __

10) 26 27 __ __ __

46

Name _____ Date _____

Finish the counting charts. Use the chart below to help you.

1	2	3	4	5	6	7	8	9	10
11	12	13	14	15	16	17	18	19	20
21	22	23	24	25	26	27	28	29	30
31	32	33	34	35	36	37	38	39	40
41	42	43	44	45	46	47	48	49	50
51	52	53	54	55	56	57	58	59	60
61	62	63	64	65	66	67	68	69	70
71	72	73	74	75	76	77	78	79	80
81	82	83	84	85	86	87	88	89	90
91	92	93	94	95	96	97	98	99	100
101	102	103	104	105	106	107	108	109	110
111	112	113	114	115	116	117	118	119	120

① | 116 | | | |

② | 99 | | | |

③ | 88 | | | |

④ | 102 | | | |

⑤ | 109 | | | |

⑥ | 62 | | | |

⑦ | 25 | | | |

⑧ | 113 | | | |

⑨ | 7 | | | |

⑩ | 96 | | | |

Name _____ Date _____

Finish the counting charts.

① | 42 | | | |

② | 28 | | | |

③ | 9 | | | |

④ | 106 | | | |

⑤ | 98 | | | |

⑥ | 49 | | | |

⑦ | 14 | | | |

⑧ | 115 | | | |

⑨ | 30 | | | |

⑩ | 14 | | | |

⑪ | 25 | | | |

⑫ | 101 | | | |

25 Common Core Math Lessons for the Interactive Whiteboard: Grade 1 © 2014 by Steve Wyborney, Scholastic Teaching Resources

Name _____ Date _____

This chart is missing some numbers. Fill in the missing numbers.

1	2	3	4	5	6	7	8	9	10
11	12	13	14	15					
21	22	23	24	25					
31	32	33	34	35					
41	42	43	44	45					
51	52	53	54	55					
61	62	63	64	65					
71	72	73	74	75					
81	82	83	84	85					
91	92	93	94	95					

Name _____ Date _____

This chart is missing some numbers. Fill in the missing numbers.

1	2	3	4	5					
					16	17	18	19	20
21	22	23	24	25					
					36	37	38	39	40
41	42	43	44	45					
					56	57	58	59	60
61	62	63	64	65					
					76	77	78	79	80
81	82	83	84	85					
					96	97	98	99	100
101	102	103	104	105					
					116	117	118	119	120

Name _____ Date _____

This chart is missing some numbers. Fill in the missing numbers.

1	2	3	4	5	6	7			
			14	15	16	17			
			24	25	26	27			
			34	35	36	37			
			44	45	46	47			
			54	55	56	57			
			64	65	66	67			
			74	75	76	77			
			84	85	86	87			
			94	95	96	97			
			104	105	106	107			
			114	115	116	117			

Name _____ Date _____

Compare the numbers. Use <, >, or =.

①   1 ◯ 2   ②   3 ◯ 2

③   4 ◯ 1   ④   5 ◯ 5

⑤   3 ◯ 6   ⑥   6 ◯ 7

⑦   5 ◯ 2   ⑧   4 ◯ 3

⑨   7 ◯ 7   ⑩   6 ◯ 5

⑪   8 ◯ 9   ⑫   9 ◯ 4

Name _____ Date _____

Compare the numbers. Use <, >, or =.

①   7 ◯ 6   ②   3 ◯ 2

③   1 ◯ 6   ④   3 ◯ 3

⑤   8 ◯ 8   ⑥   1 ◯ 7

⑦   3 ◯ 9   ⑧   7 ◯ 5

⑨   4 ◯ 4   ⑩   7 ◯ 8

⑪   2 ◯ 9   ⑫   9 ◯ 2

Understanding Comparison Symbols: C

Name _____ Date _____

Compare the numbers. Use <, >, or =.

① 2 ◯ 7

② 6 ◯ 5

③ 9 ◯ 9

④ 1 ◯ 1

⑤ 4 ◯ 8

⑥ 8 ◯ 9

⑦ 2 ◯ 2

⑧ 4 ◯ 5

⑨ 7 ◯ 1

⑩ 3 ◯ 4

⑪ 6 ◯ 2

⑫ 8 ◯ 8

54

25 Common Core Math Lessons for the Interactive Whiteboard: Grade 1 © 2014 by Steve Wyborney, Scholastic Teaching Resources

Name _____ Date _____

Compare the numbers. Use <, >, or =.

① 25 ◯ 25

② 10 ◯ 11

③ 22 ◯ 23

④ 32 ◯ 31

⑤ 46 ◯ 45

⑥ 38 ◯ 39

⑦ 26 ◯ 27

⑧ 45 ◯ 41

⑨ 72 ◯ 71

⑩ 54 ◯ 51

⑪ 76 ◯ 71

⑫ 87 ◯ 89

Name _____ Date _____

Compare the numbers. Use <, >, or =.

① 11 ◯ 10   ② 12 ◯ 19

③ 13 ◯ 25   ④ 21 ◯ 17

⑤ 31 ◯ 22   ⑥ 61 ◯ 45

⑦ 28 ◯ 54   ⑧ 73 ◯ 19

⑨ 58 ◯ 49   ⑩ 16 ◯ 16

⑪ 64 ◯ 93   ⑫ 56 ◯ 56

25 Common Core Math Lessons for the Interactive Whiteboard: Grade 1 © 2014 by Steve Wyborney, Scholastic Teaching Resources

Name _____ Date _____

Compare the numbers. Use <, >, or =.

① 32 ◯ 35

② 17 ◯ 19

③ 54 ◯ 51

④ 8 ◯ 18

⑤ 52 ◯ 32

⑥ 26 ◯ 31

⑦ 49 ◯ 50

⑧ 78 ◯ 82

⑨ 15 ◯ 3

⑩ 6 ◯ 24

⑪ 23 ◯ 72

⑫ 55 ◯ 60

25 Common Core Math Lessons for the Interactive Whiteboard: Grade 1 © 2014 by Steve Wyborney, Scholastic Teaching Resources

Name _____ Date _____

Find the sum. Use the hundreds chart to help you.

1	2	3	4	5	6	7	8	9	10
11	12	13	14	15	16	17	18	19	20
21	22	23	24	25	26	27	28	29	30
31	32	33	34	35	36	37	38	39	40
41	42	43	44	45	46	47	48	49	50
51	52	53	54	55	56	57	58	59	60
61	62	63	64	65	66	67	68	69	70
71	72	73	74	75	76	77	78	79	80
81	82	83	84	85	86	87	88	89	90
91	92	93	94	95	96	97	98	99	100

① $14 + 5 =$ _____   ② $15 + 6 =$ _____

③ $11 + 5 =$ _____   ④ $22 + 6 =$ _____

⑤ $27 + 8 =$ _____   ⑥ $35 + 7 =$ _____

⑦ $41 + 8 =$ _____   ⑧ $56 + 9 =$ _____

⑨ $64 + 6 =$ _____   ⑩ $73 + 9 =$ _____

⑪ $81 + 7 =$ _____   ⑫ $93 + 6 =$ _____

25 Common Core Math Lessons for the Interactive Whiteboard: Grade 1 © 2014 by Steve Wyborney, Scholastic Teaching Resources

Name _____ Date _____

Find the sum. Use the hundreds chart to help you.

1	2	3	4	5	6	7	8	9	10
11	12	13	14	15	16	17	18	19	20
21	22	23	24	25	26	27	28	29	30
31	32	33	34	35	36	37	38	39	40
41	42	43	44	45	46	47	48	49	50
51	52	53	54	55	56	57	58	59	60
61	62	63	64	65	66	67	68	69	70
71	72	73	74	75	76	77	78	79	80
81	82	83	84	85	86	87	88	89	90
91	92	93	94	95	96	97	98	99	100

① $18 + 6 =$ _____   ② $23 + 9 =$ _____

③ $34 + 7 =$ _____   ④ $39 + 4 =$ _____

⑤ $41 + 5 =$ _____   ⑥ $49 + 5 =$ _____

⑦ $52 + 8 =$ _____   ⑧ $67 + 5 =$ _____

⑨ $73 + 4 =$ _____   ⑩ $76 + 9 =$ _____

⑪ $84 + 7 =$ _____   ⑫ $95 + 3 =$ _____

Name _____ Date _____

Find the sum. Use the hundreds chart to help you.

1	2	3	4	5	6	7	8	9	10
11	12	13	14	15	16	17	18	19	20
21	22	23	24	25	26	27	28	29	30
31	32	33	34	35	36	37	38	39	40
41	42	43	44	45	46	47	48	49	50
51	52	53	54	55	56	57	58	59	60
61	62	63	64	65	66	67	68	69	70
71	72	73	74	75	76	77	78	79	80
81	82	83	84	85	86	87	88	89	90
91	92	93	94	95	96	97	98	99	100

① $13 + 9 =$ _____

② $21 + 7 =$ _____

③ $28 + 4 =$ _____

④ $35 + 6 =$ _____

⑤ $38 + 3 =$ _____

⑥ $41 + 7 =$ _____

⑦ $49 + 9 =$ _____

⑧ $53 + 6 =$ _____

⑨ $65 + 5 =$ _____

⑩ $78 + 5 =$ _____

⑪ $88 + 8 =$ _____

⑫ $96 + 4 =$ _____

25 Common Core Math Lessons for the Interactive Whiteboard: Grade 1 © 2014 by Steve Wyborney, Scholastic Teaching Resources

Name _____ Date _____

Find the sum. Use the hundreds chart to help you.

1	2	3	4	5	6	7	8	9	10
11	12	13	14	15	16	17	18	19	20
21	22	23	24	25	26	27	28	29	30
31	32	33	34	35	36	37	38	39	40
41	42	43	44	45	46	47	48	49	50
51	52	53	54	55	56	57	58	59	60
61	62	63	64	65	66	67	68	69	70
71	72	73	74	75	76	77	78	79	80
81	82	83	84	85	86	87	88	89	90
91	92	93	94	95	96	97	98	99	100

① $7 + 10 =$ _____   ② $5 + 30 =$ _____

③ $9 + 40 =$ _____   ④ $3 + 50 =$ _____

⑤ $11 + 30 =$ _____   ⑥ $15 + 60 =$ _____

⑦ $19 + 40 =$ _____   ⑧ $21 + 60 =$ _____

⑨ $23 + 40 =$ _____   ⑩ $25 + 70 =$ _____

⑪ $28 + 20 =$ _____   ⑫ $30 + 70 =$ _____

Name _____ Date _____

Find the sum. Use the hundreds chart to help you.

1	2	3	4	5	6	7	8	9	10
11	12	13	14	15	16	17	18	19	20
21	22	23	24	25	26	27	28	29	30
31	32	33	34	35	36	37	38	39	40
41	42	43	44	45	46	47	48	49	50
51	52	53	54	55	56	57	58	59	60
61	62	63	64	65	66	67	68	69	70
71	72	73	74	75	76	77	78	79	80
81	82	83	84	85	86	87	88	89	90
91	92	93	94	95	96	97	98	99	100

① $8 + 10 =$ _____

② $15 + 30 =$ _____

③ $23 + 40 =$ _____

④ $29 + 60 =$ _____

⑤ $34 + 50 =$ _____

⑥ $37 + 20 =$ _____

⑦ $41 + 10 =$ _____

⑧ $48 + 50 =$ _____

⑨ $51 + 20 =$ _____

⑩ $65 + 30 =$ _____

⑪ $71 + 10 =$ _____

⑫ $86 + 10 =$ _____

Name _____ Date _____

Find the sum. Use the hundreds chart to help you.

1	2	3	4	5	6	7	8	9	10
11	12	13	14	15	16	17	18	19	20
21	22	23	24	25	26	27	28	29	30
31	32	33	34	35	36	37	38	39	40
41	42	43	44	45	46	47	48	49	50
51	52	53	54	55	56	57	58	59	60
61	62	63	64	65	66	67	68	69	70
71	72	73	74	75	76	77	78	79	80
81	82	83	84	85	86	87	88	89	90
91	92	93	94	95	96	97	98	99	100

① 24 + 10 = _____

② 6 + 20 = _____

③ 31 + 30 = _____

④ 25 + 20 = _____

⑤ 30 + 40 = _____

⑥ 42 + 50 = _____

⑦ 10 + 60 = _____

⑧ 8 + 50 = _____

⑨ 17 + 70 = _____

⑩ 32 + 40 = _____

⑪ 84 + 10 = _____

⑫ 63 + 30 = _____

Name _____ Date _____

Find the difference. Use the hundreds chart to help you.

1	2	3	4	5	6	7	8	9	10
11	12	13	14	15	16	17	18	19	20
21	22	23	24	25	26	27	28	29	30
31	32	33	34	35	36	37	38	39	40
41	42	43	44	45	46	47	48	49	50
51	52	53	54	55	56	57	58	59	60
61	62	63	64	65	66	67	68	69	70
71	72	73	74	75	76	77	78	79	80
81	82	83	84	85	86	87	88	89	90
91	92	93	94	95	96	97	98	99	100

① $50 - 10 =$ _____   ② $20 - 10 =$ _____

③ $70 - 10 =$ _____   ④ $50 - 20 =$ _____

⑤ $80 - 30 =$ _____   ⑥ $90 - 20 =$ _____

⑦ $70 - 60 =$ _____   ⑧ $40 - 30 =$ _____

⑨ $80 - 60 =$ _____   ⑩ $70 - 40 =$ _____

⑪ $60 - 10 =$ _____   ⑫ $90 - 30 =$ _____

Name _____ Date _____

Find the difference. Use the hundreds chart to help you.

1	2	3	4	5	6	7	8	9	10
11	12	13	14	15	16	17	18	19	20
21	22	23	24	25	26	27	28	29	30
31	32	33	34	35	36	37	38	39	40
41	42	43	44	45	46	47	48	49	50
51	52	53	54	55	56	57	58	59	60
61	62	63	64	65	66	67	68	69	70
71	72	73	74	75	76	77	78	79	80
81	82	83	84	85	86	87	88	89	90
91	92	93	94	95	96	97	98	99	100

① $60 - 10 =$ _____   ② $80 - 20 =$ _____

③ $70 - 30 =$ _____   ④ $90 - 80 =$ _____

⑤ $80 - 10 =$ _____   ⑥ $60 - 30 =$ _____

⑦ $40 - 30 =$ _____   ⑧ $50 - 10 =$ _____

⑨ $40 - 20 =$ _____   ⑩ $50 - 30 =$ _____

⑪ $90 - 30 =$ _____   ⑫ $80 - 60 =$ _____

Subtracting Multiples of 10: C

Name _____ Date _____

Find the difference. Use the hundreds chart to help you.

1	2	3	4	5	6	7	8	9	10
11	12	13	14	15	16	17	18	19	20
21	22	23	24	25	26	27	28	29	30
31	32	33	34	35	36	37	38	39	40
41	42	43	44	45	46	47	48	49	50
51	52	53	54	55	56	57	58	59	60
61	62	63	64	65	66	67	68	69	70
71	72	73	74	75	76	77	78	79	80
81	82	83	84	85	86	87	88	89	90
91	92	93	94	95	96	97	98	99	100

① 81 – 10 = _____

② 61 – 20 = _____

③ 91 – 30 = _____

④ 72 – 40 = _____

⑤ 62 – 10 = _____

⑥ 25 – 20 = _____

⑦ 44 – 30 = _____

⑧ 100 – 70 = _____

⑨ 92 – 50 = _____

⑩ 80 – 50 = _____

⑪ 50 – 10 = _____

⑫ 48 – 30 = _____

Name _____ Date _____

What number is 10 more? Write it in the top box.
What number is 10 less? Write it in the bottom box.
The first one has been done for you.

40	☐	☐
① 30	② 50	③ 40
20	☐	☐

☐	☐	☐
④ 70	⑤ 60	⑥ 80
☐	☐	☐

☐	☐	☐
⑦ 20	⑧ 90	⑨ 41
☐	☐	☐

☐	☐	☐
⑩ 81	⑪ 21	⑫ 51
☐	☐	☐

Name _____ Date _____

What number is 10 more? Write it in the top box.
What number is 10 less? Write it in the bottom box.
The first one has been done for you.

① | 60 |
50
| 40 |

② | |
90
| |

③ | |
40
| |

④ | |
80
| |

⑤ | |
30
| |

⑥ | |
70
| |

⑦ | |
20
| |

⑧ | |
60
| |

⑨ | |
45
| |

⑩ | |
85
| |

⑪ | |
15
| |

⑫ | |
55
| |

25 Common Core Math Lessons for the Interactive Whiteboard: Grade 1 © 2014 by Steve Wyborney, Scholastic Teaching Resources

Name _____ Date _____

**What number is 10 more? Write it in the top box.
What number is 10 less? Write it in the bottom box.
The first one has been done for you.**

52

① 42

32

② 85

③ 17

④ 37

⑤ 51

⑥ 64

⑦ 28

⑧ 14

⑨ 70

⑩ 52

⑪ 64

⑫ 45

Name _____ Date _____

How many units long is each shape?

1 unit

①

_____ units

②

_____ units

③

_____ units

④

_____ units

Name _____ Date _____

How many units long is each shape?

1 unit

① _____ units

② _____ units

③ _____ units

④ _____ units

⑤ _____ units

⑥ _____ units

⑦ _____ units

⑧ _____ units

Name _____ Date _____

How many units long is each shape?

1 unit

↔

① _____ units

② _____ units

③ _____ units

④ _____ units

⑤ _____ units

⑥ _____ units

⑦ _____ units

⑧ _____ units

Name _____ Date _____

Which shape is longer? Circle the shape that is longer.

① A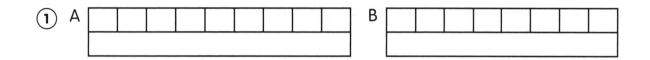

② A

③ A

④ A

⑤ A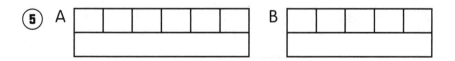

⑥ A B

25 Common Core Math Lessons for the Interactive Whiteboard: Grade 1 © 2014 by Steve Wyborney, Scholastic Teaching Resources

Name _____ Date _____

Which shape is longer? Circle the shape that is longer.

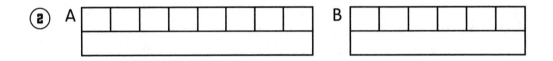

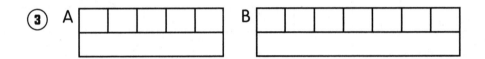

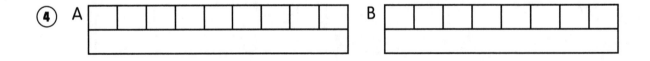

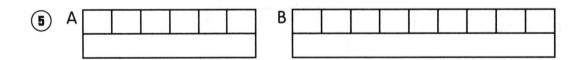

Name _____ Date _____

Which shape is longer? Circle the shape that is longer.

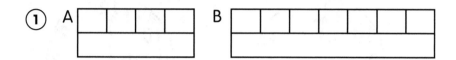

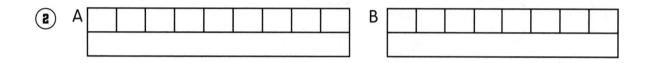

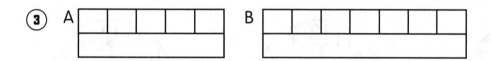

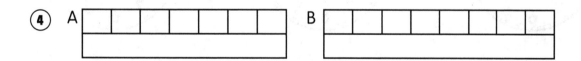

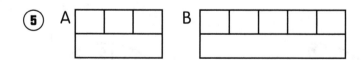

Name _____ Date _____

Write the time shown on each clock. The first one has been done for you.

① __4:00__

② _____

③ _____

④ _____

⑤ _____

⑥ _____

⑦ _____

⑧ _____

⑨ _____

Name _____ Date _____

Write the time shown on each clock. The first one has been done for you.

① ___7:00___

② _____

③ _____

④ _____

⑤ _____

⑥ _____

⑦ _____

⑧ _____

⑨ _____

Name _____ Date _____

Write the time shown on each clock. The first one has been done for you.

① *9:00*   **②** _____   **③** _____

④ _____   **⑤** _____   **⑥** _____

⑦ _____   **⑧** _____   **⑨** _____

25 Common Core Math Lessons for the Interactive Whiteboard: Grade 1 © 2014 by Steve Wyborney, Scholastic Teaching Resources

Name _____ Date _____

Write the time shown on each clock. The first one has been done for you.

(1) ___7:30___

(2) _____

(3) _____

(4) _____

(5) _____

(6) _____

(7) _____

(8) _____

(9) _____

Name _____ Date _____

Write the time shown on each clock. The first one has been done for you.

1. 2:30

2. _____

3. _____

4. _____

5. _____

6. _____

7. _____

8. _____

9. _____

Name _____ Date _____

Write the time shown on each clock. The first one has been done for you.

① __10:30__

② _____

③ _____

④ _____

⑤ _____

⑥ _____

⑦ _____

⑧ _____

⑨ _____

Making Shapes: A

Name _____ Date _____

Some shapes are shown below. They have extra shapes next to them. Make a new shape by tracing the extra shapes.

①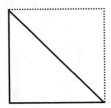

②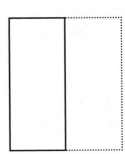

③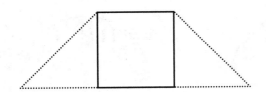

④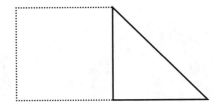

⑤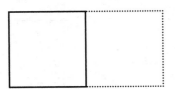

⑥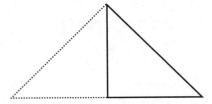

⑦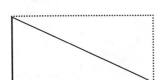

⑧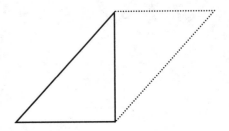

Name _____ Date _____

**Some shapes are shown below. They have extra shapes next to them.
Make a new shape by tracing the extra shapes.**

①

②

③

④

⑤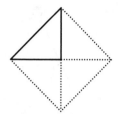

⑥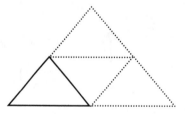

⑦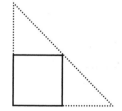

⑧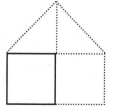

Name _____ Date _____

Break the shapes below apart. Draw lines to connect the dots. The lines will break each shape into smaller shapes.

①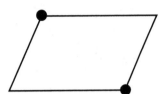

②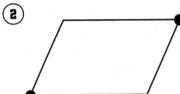

③

④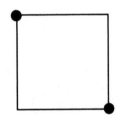

⑤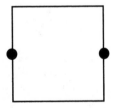

⑥

⑦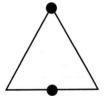

⑧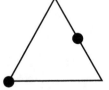

Name _____ Date _____

Break the shapes into halves. Draw a line. Use the dots as a guide.

①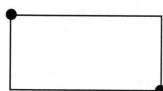

②

③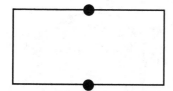

④

⑤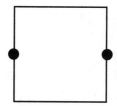

⑥

⑦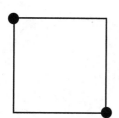

⑧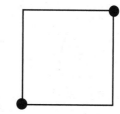

Name _____ Date _____

Break the shapes into halves. Draw a line. Use the dots as a guide.

①

②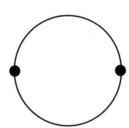

③

④

⑤

⑥

⑦

⑧

Name _____ Date _____

Color one half of the whole shape. The first one has been done for you.

(1)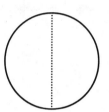

(2)

(3)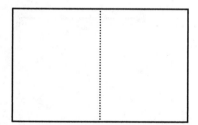

(4)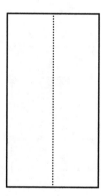

(5)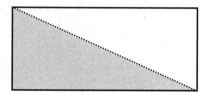

(6)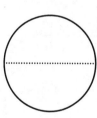

(7)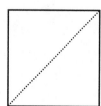

(8)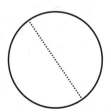

Name _____ Date _____

**Break the shapes into fourths. Draw lines. Use the dots as a guide.
Some have been done for you.**

①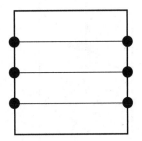

②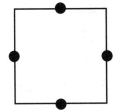

③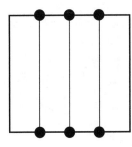

④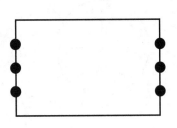

⑤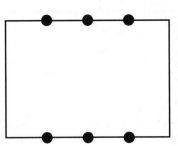

⑥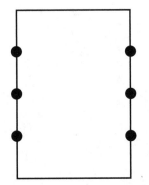

⑦

⑧

88

Name _____ Date _____

**Break the shapes into fourths. Draw lines. Use the dots as a guide.
The first one has been done for you.**

①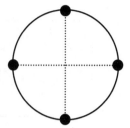

②

③

④

⑤

⑥

⑦

⑧

Name _____ Date _____

Color one fourth of the whole shape. The first one has been done for you.

①

②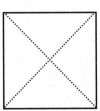

③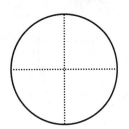

④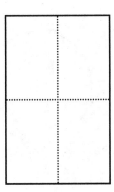

⑤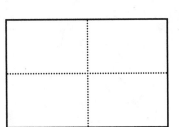

⑥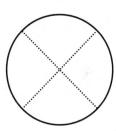

⑦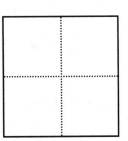

⑧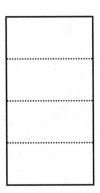

Answer Key

Counting Sets

A (p. 16): Make sure students number the shapes in the correct sequence.
B (p. 17): Make sure students number the shapes in the correct sequence.
C (p. 18): Make sure students number the shapes in the correct sequence.

Relating Counting to Addition

A (p. 19): **1.** 7 **2.** 11 **3.** 8 **4.** 6
B (p. 20): **1.** 8 **2.** 9 **3.** 8 **4.** 11
C (p. 21): **1.** 13 **2.** 12 **3.** 14 **4.** 13

Relating Counting to Subtraction

A (p. 22): **1.** 3 **2.** 1 **3.** 2 **4.** 2 **5.** 7 **6.** 5 **7.** 3 **8.** 2
B (p. 23): **1.** 3 **2.** 4 **3.** 2 **4.** 8 **5.** 4 **6.** 9
C (p. 24): **1.** 11 **2.** 7 **3.** 3 **4.** 6 **5.** 8 **6.** 6

The Commutative Property of Addition

A (p. 25): **1.** 8 **2.** 5 **3.** 9 **4.** 3 **5.** 7 **6.** 6 **7.** 4 **8.** 5
9. 9 **10.** 8
B (p. 26): **1.** 14 **2.** 11 **3.** 7 **4.** 16 **5.** 9 **6.** 12 **7.** 17
8. 10 **9.** 14 **10.** 16
C (p. 27): **1.** 14 **2.** 14 **3.** 15 **4.** 7 **5.** 9 **6.** 17 **7.** 11
8. 19 **9.** 12 **10.** 12

Using a Number Line to Add Two Numbers

A (p. 28): **1.** 9 **2.** 8 **3.** 7 **4.** 11 **5.** 14 **6.** 13 **7.** 14 **8.** 7
9. 11 **10.** 12 **11.** 18 **12.** 12
B (p. 29): **1.** 16 **2.** 13 **3.** 15 **4.** 18 **5.** 14 **6.** 12 **7.** 16
8. 15 **9.** 18 **10.** 10 **11.** 11 **12.** 19
C (p. 30): **1.** 18 **2.** 20 **3.** 19 **4.** 15 **5.** 17 **6.** 19 **7.** 16
8. 15 **9.** 13 **10.** 17 **11.** 18 **12.** 20

Using a Number Line to Subtract

A (p. 31): **1.** 3 **2.** 5 **3.** 1 **4.** 2 **5.** 8 **6.** 9 **7.** 7 **8.** 2
9. 12 **10.** 6 **11.** 4 **12.** 11
B (p. 32): **1.** 13 **2.** 3 **3.** 2 **4.** 3 **5.** 5 **6.** 4 **7.** 10 **8.** 3
9. 12 **10.** 7 **11.** 12 **12.** 11
C (p. 33): **1.** 11 **2.** 1 **3.** 5 **4.** 7 **5.** 4 **6.** 8 **7.** 3 **8.** 15
9. 6 **10.** 2 **11.** 14 **12.** 5

Using a Number Line to Add Three Numbers

A (p. 34): **1.** 9 **2.** 15 **3.** 13 **4.** 11 **5.** 15 **6.** 15 **7.** 17
8. 19 **9.** 8 **10.** 20 **11.** 13 **12.** 10
B (p. 35): **1.** 20 **2.** 12 **3.** 18 **4.** 19 **5.** 17 **6.** 7 **7.** 17
8. 20 **9.** 15 **10.** 13 **11.** 12 **12.** 9
C (p. 36): **1.** 9 **2.** 17 **3.** 18 **4.** 19 **5.** 13 **6.** 15 **7.** 15
8. 11 **9.** 7 **10.** 17 **11.** 16 **12.** 7

Reading & Writing Numbers Through 120

A (p. 37): Make sure students trace the numbers correctly.
B (p. 38): Make sure students trace the numbers correctly.
C (p. 39): **1.** 46 **2.** 21 **3.** 75 **4.** 52 **5.** 91 **6.** 103 **7.** 76
8. 69 **9.** 84 **10.** 112 **11.** 27 **12.** 56

Understanding Ones and Tens Through 19

A (p. 40): **1.** 12 **2.** 14 **3.** 19 **4.** 11 **5.** 18 **6.** 17 **7.** 13
8. 16 **9.** 15
B (p. 41): **1.** 14 **2.** 18 **3.** 17 **4.** 19 **5.** 12 **6.** 15 **7.** 11
8. 16 **9.** 13
C (p. 42): **1.** 18 **2.** 15 **3.** 12 **4.** 17 **5.** 19 **6.** 13 **7.** 14
8. 11 **9.** 16

Understanding Ones and Tens in Larger Numbers

A (p. 43): **1.** 28 **2.** 15 **3.** 34 **4.** 24 **5.** 31 **6.** 17 **7.** 26
8. 37 **9.** 29
B (p. 44): **1.** 27 **2.** 12 **3.** 34 **4.** 52 **5.** 41 **6.** 33 **7.** 45
C (p. 45): **1.** 38 **2.** 23 **3.** 45 **4.** 64 **5.** 57 **6.** 43 **7.** 56

Counting Sequences Between 1 and 120

A (p. 46): **1.** 23, 24, 25 **2.** 40, 41, 42 **3.** 11, 12, 13 **4.** 79,
80, 81 **5.** 47, 48, 49 **6.** 55, 56, 57 **7.** 89, 90, 91 **8.** 39,
40, 41 **9.** 15, 16, 17 **10.** 28, 29, 30
B (p. 47): **1.** 117, 118, 119, 120 **2.** 100, 101, 102, 103
3. 89, 90, 91, 92 **4.** 103, 104, 105, 106 **5.** 110, 111, 112,
113 **6.** 63, 64, 65, 66 **7.** 26, 27, 28, 29 **8.** 114, 115, 116,
117 **9.** 8, 9, 10, 11 **10.** 97, 98, 99, 100
C (p. 48): **1.** 43, 44, 45, 46 **2.** 29, 30, 31, 32 **3.** 10, 11,
12, 13 **4.** 107, 108, 109, 110 **5.** 99, 100, 101, 102 **6.** 50,
51, 52, 53 **7.** 15, 16, 17, 18 **8.** 116, 117, 118, 119 **9.** 31,
32, 33, 34 **10.** 15, 16, 17, 18 **11.** 26, 27, 28, 29 **12.** 102,
103, 104, 105

Counting to 120 From Any Number

A (p. 49), **B** (p. 50), **C** (p. 51): Make sure students fill the
spaces with the correct numbers.

1	2	3	4	5	6	7	8	9	10
11	12	13	14	15	16	17	18	19	20
21	22	23	24	25	26	27	28	29	30
31	32	33	34	35	36	37	38	39	40
41	42	43	44	45	46	47	48	49	50
51	52	53	54	55	56	57	58	59	60
61	62	63	64	65	66	67	68	69	70
71	72	73	74	75	76	77	78	79	80
81	82	83	84	85	86	87	88	89	90
91	92	93	94	95	96	97	98	99	100
101	102	103	104	105	106	107	108	109	110
111	112	113	114	115	116	117	118	119	120

Understanding Comparison Symbols
A (p. 52): **1.** < **2.** > **3.** > **4.** = **5.** < **6.** < **7.** > **8.** >
9. = **10.** > **11.** < **12.** >
B (p. 53): **1.** > **2.** > **3.** < **4.** = **5.** = **6.** < **7.** < **8.** >
9. = **10.** < **11.** < **12.** >
C (p. 54): **1.** < **2.** > **3.** = **4.** = **5.** < **6.** < **7.** = **8.** <
9. > **10.** < **11.** > **12.** =

Comparing Two-Digit Numbers
A (p. 55): **1.** = **2.** < **3.** < **4.** > **5.** > **6.** < **7.** < **8.** >
9. > **10.** > **11.** > **12.** <
B (p. 56): **1.** > **2.** < **3.** < **4.** > **5.** > **6.** > **7.** < **8.** >
9. > **10.** = **11.** < **12.** =
C (p. 57): **1.** < **2.** < **3.** > **4.** < **5.** > **6.** < **7.** < **8.** <
9. > **10.** < **11.** < **12.** <

Adding a One-Digit Number to a Two-Digit Number
A (p. 58): **1.** 19 **2.** 21 **3.** 16 **4.** 28 **5.** 35 **6.** 42 **7.** 49
8. 65 **9.** 70 **10.** 82 **11.** 88 **12.** 99
B (p. 59): **1.** 24 **2.** 32 **3.** 41 **4.** 43 **5.** 46 **6.** 54 **7.** 60
8. 72 **9.** 77 **10.** 85 **11.** 91 **12.** 98
C (p. 60): **1.** 22 **2.** 28 **3.** 32 **4.** 41 **5.** 41 **6.** 48 **7.** 58
8. 59 **9.** 70 **10.** 83 **11.** 96 **12.** 100

Adding Multiples of 10
A (p. 61): **1.** 17 **2.** 35 **3.** 49 **4.** 53 **5.** 41 **6.** 75 **7.** 59
8. 81 **9.** 63 **10.** 95 **11.** 48 **12.** 100
B (p. 62): **1.** 18 **2.** 45 **3.** 63 **4.** 89 **5.** 84 **6.** 57 **7.** 51
8. 98 **9.** 71 **10.** 95 **11.** 81 **12.** 96
C (p. 63): **1.** 34 **2.** 26 **3.** 61 **4.** 45 **5.** 70 **6.** 92 **7.** 70
8. 58 **9.** 87 **10.** 72 **11.** 94 **12.** 93

Subtracting Multiples of 10
A (p. 64): **1.** 40 **2.** 10 **3.** 60 **4.** 30 **5.** 50 **6.** 70 **7.** 10
8. 10 **9.** 20 **10.** 30 **11.** 50 **12.** 60
B (p. 65): **1.** 50 **2.** 60 **3.** 40 **4.** 10 **5.** 70 **6.** 30 **7.** 10
8. 40 **9.** 20 **10.** 20 **11.** 60 **12.** 20
C (p. 66): **1.** 71 **2.** 41 **3.** 61 **4.** 32 **5.** 52 **6.** 5 **7.** 14
8. 30 **9.** 42 **10.** 30 **11.** 40 **12.** 18

Mentally Adding & Subtracting
A (p. 67): **2.** 60, 40 **3.** 50, 30 **4.** 80, 60 **5.** 70, 50
6. 90, 70 **7.** 30, 10 **8.** 100, 80 **9.** 51, 31 **10.** 91, 71
11. 31, 11 **12.** 61, 41
B (p. 68): **2.** 100, 80 **3.** 50, 30 **4.** 90, 70 **5.** 40, 20
6. 80, 60 **7.** 30, 10 **8.** 70, 50 **9.** 55, 35 **10.** 95, 75
11. 25, 5 **12.** 65, 45
C (p. 69): **2.** 95, 75 **3.** 27, 7 **4.** 47, 27 **5.** 61, 41
6. 74, 54 **7.** 38, 18 **8.** 24, 4 **9.** 80, 60 **10.** 62, 42
11. 74, 54 **12.** 55, 35

Measuring Length
A (p. 70): **1.** 4 units **2.** 7 units **3.** 5 units **4.** 6 units
B (p. 71): **1.** 8 units **2.** 4 units **3.** 7 units **4.** 3 units
5. 2 units **6.** 9 units **7.** 5 units **8.** 6 units
C (p. 72): **1.** 10 units **2.** 2 units **3.** 7 units **4.** 5 units
5. 8 units **6.** 3 units **7.** 4 units **8.** 6 units

Comparing Length
A (p. 73): **1.** A **2.** B **3.** B **4.** B **5.** A **6.** A
B (p. 74): **1.** B **2.** A **3.** B **4.** A **5.** B **6.** B
C (p. 75): **1.** B **2.** A **3.** B **4.** B **5.** B **6.** B

Reading Analog Clocks to the Nearest Hour
A (p. 76): **2.** 2:00 **3.** 9:00 **4.** 6:00 **5.** 3:00 **6.** 8:00
7. 1:00 **8.** 5:00 **9.** 11:00
B (p. 77): **2.** 10:00 **3.** 1:00 **4.** 5:00 **5.** 11:00 **6.** 3:00
7. 6:00 **8.** 12:00 **9.** 9:00
C (p. 78): **2.** 4:00 **3.** 2:00 **4.** 10:00 **5.** 5:00 **6.** 1:00
7. 7:00 **8.** 8:00 **9.** 3:00

Reading Analog Clocks to the Nearest Half Hour
A (p. 79): **2.** 2:30 **3.** 10:30 **4.** 1:30 **5.** 6:30 **6.** 3:30
7. 11:30 **8.** 5:30 **9.** 4:30
B (p. 80): **2.** 11:30 **3.** 1:30 **4.** 12:30 **5.** 3:30 **6.** 9:30
7. 4:30 **8.** 5:30 **9.** 6:30
C (p. 81): **2.** 1:30 **3.** 5:30 **4.** 8:30 **5.** 4:30 **6.** 7:30
7. 6:30 **8.** 9:30 **9.** 3:30

Making Shapes
A (p. 82): Make sure students trace the shapes correctly.
B (p. 83): Make sure students trace the shapes correctly.
C (p. 84): Make sure students draw the lines correctly.

Partitioning Shapes Into Halves
A (p. 85): Make sure students draw the lines correctly.
B (p. 86): Make sure students draw the lines correctly.
C (p. 87): Make sure students color one half of each shape.

Partitioning Shapes Into Fourths
A (p. 88): Make sure students draw the lines correctly.
B (p. 89): Make sure students draw the lines correctly.
C (p. 90): Make sure students color one fourth of each shape.